# Cut-Out Fun with Matisse

Make your own cut-outs
like Matisse!

Prestel

In the town of Nice on the French Riviera there is a very old building called the Hotel Régina. People say that there are strange goings-on in a certain room on the third floor . . . Sometimes, if you listen at the door, you can hear the oddest sounds and the light often stays on late into the night. A few months ago, an old man with a white beard moved in there. His name is Henri Matisse and he has just discovered something amazing—how to draw with scissors!

He is sitting in a wheelchair in his room, with paper scattered around him all over the floor, cutting out shapes—wonderful shapes—from huge sheets of coloured paper. Large, small, curved, wavy, round, pointed, zigzag shapes, squares, hearts, crosses, stars, leaves, crescents, apples, seaweed shapes, letters of the alphabet . . . every possible shape you can imagine. He has taken off his shoes and is shuffling the pieces of paper around on the floor with his bare feet to get a better look at them, arranging them with his toes, and all the while snipping away with his scissors.

snip-snip, snippety-snip

The walls of the room are covered with hundreds of cut-out shapes in patterns that go all the way up to the ceiling. "Drawing with scissors . . . cutting directly into colour . . ." mumbles Matisse, stopping for a moment to straighten a few particularly well-cut blue shapes on the wall.

He likes what he sees.

3

Lost in thought, Matisse gazes at the shapes he has made.

Suddenly, the wall seems to flicker before his very eyes. Everything begins to blur. The blue paper shapes move all by themselves. A graceful young woman, wearing not a stitch of clothing, sits down in front of Matisse. She crosses her legs and looks him straight in the eye.

"Henri," she says in a quiet, gentle voice: "You have drawn me and painted me many times. And yet I hardly know you. Tell me, what is your greatest wish?"

Matisse thinks for a moment and says: "To see the world through the eyes of a child."

The woman smiles. "The answer lies in your hands."

"What do you mean?" asks Matisse. Then he looks down and sees the scissors in his hand and starts snipping away again, cutting shapes out of the coloured paper, getting better and better all the time.

. . . snip-snip, snippety-snip . . .

Quietly, rhythmically: snip-snip, snippety-snip . . . almost like a melody played on piano, saxophone and drums. Everything in the room seems to move to the beat, even the paper shapes on the wall.

The young woman is no longer sitting cross-legged on the floor.
She has stood up and has begun to dance to the music.

She swings her legs up over her head like an acrobat, then she
takes a blue rope and sweeps it up over her head and down
again beneath her feet. She is hopping and skipping in a graceful
dance.

Soon, the walls of the room are too small for her, and her
skipping rope keeps catching on the door frame and pieces
of furniture.

Things are happening on the opposite wall, too. With a whoop of joy, another dancer leaps up and turns a cartwheel. She moves so fast across her orange mat that we just catch a glimpse of her black legs and arms among the white feathers of her dress.

Nearby, above a dark wooden chest of drawers and behind the flowers, something else is moving. Two large shapes—it's hard to tell whether they are figures or statues or even spinning tops or vases—start swaying to the rhythm of the music. It is not easy for them to keep their balance. The silvery-white shape on the left is a little lighter and more supple. The blue shape on the right is heavier and has difficulty keeping up with the figure on the left.

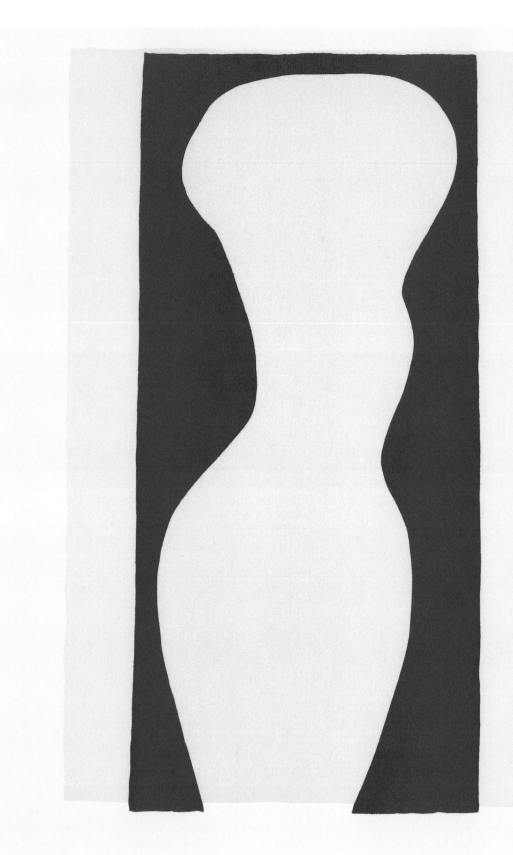

Matisse can hardly
believe his eyes. After
a while, it all gets too
much for him.

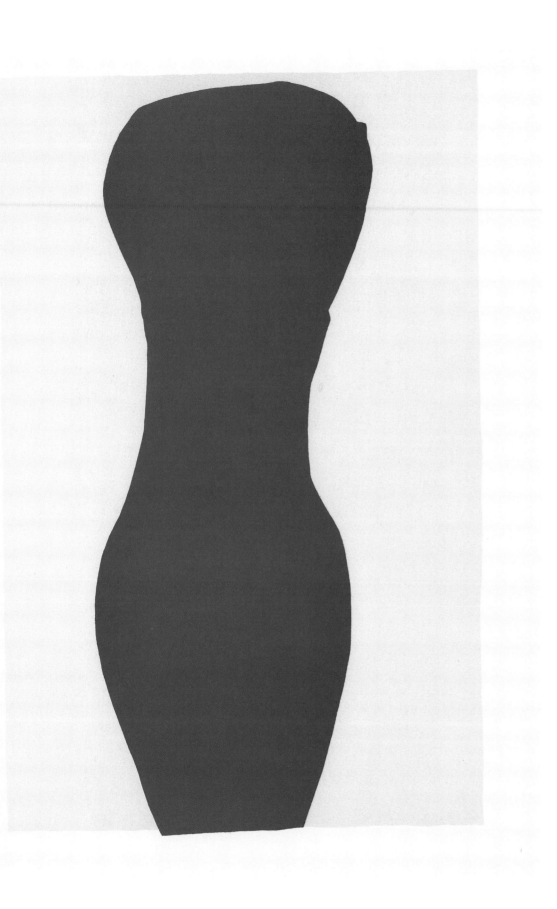

"Stop! Enough of that!
My curved lines are not
so wild. All cut-outs
go back to your places
now—exactly where
I put you!"

Luckily, he remembers that he cut out a bell shape for the top corner of the room not so long ago. He takes a good look at the bell, trims it a little with a quick snip-snip of his scissors, until it is just right—and suddenly it gives out a long, loud peal like a gong.

At the sound of the bell, everything goes quiet.

Next morning, Matisse is feeling a little tired after all the excitement of the night before. He is a frail old man, even though he is full of the joys of life. He decides to sit up in bed to do some drawing with the help of a long stick. He ties a piece of chalk to the end of it and traces the outline of a face on the wall.

As he does so, he thinks how wonderful it would be to travel to the South Seas instead of sitting here in bed. And then he remembers: "The answer lies in your hands" . . . and he picks up the scissors from his bedside table.

. . . snip-snip, snippety-snip . . .

The room is getting warmer. A pleasantly heavy, tropical breeze wafts through the window. The wonderful smell of flowers fills the room and there is a quiet buzz in the air. Suddenly, a swarm of bees flies over Matisse and his bed in a shimmering, vibrant cloud of red, blue and yellow. The bees sweep round in a huge arch across the wall of the room and fly away as a soft, warm rain begins to fall.

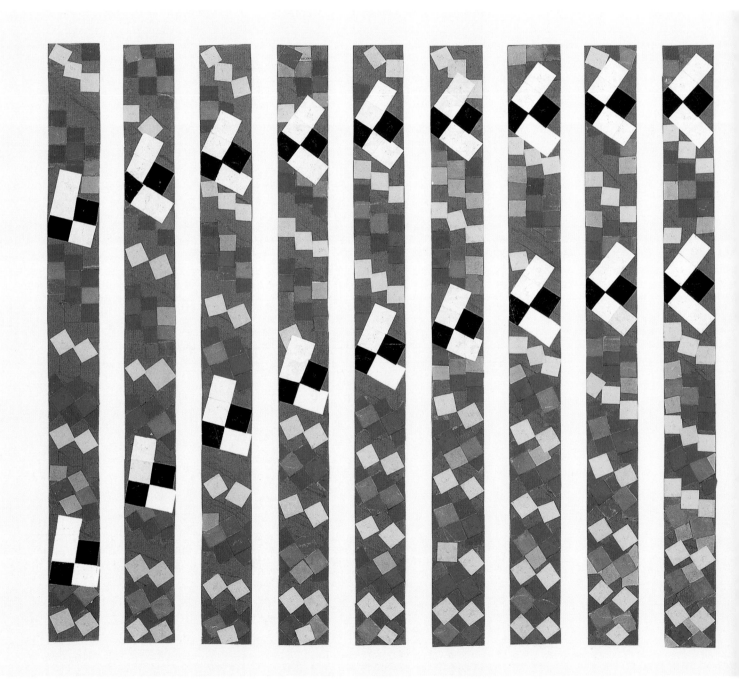

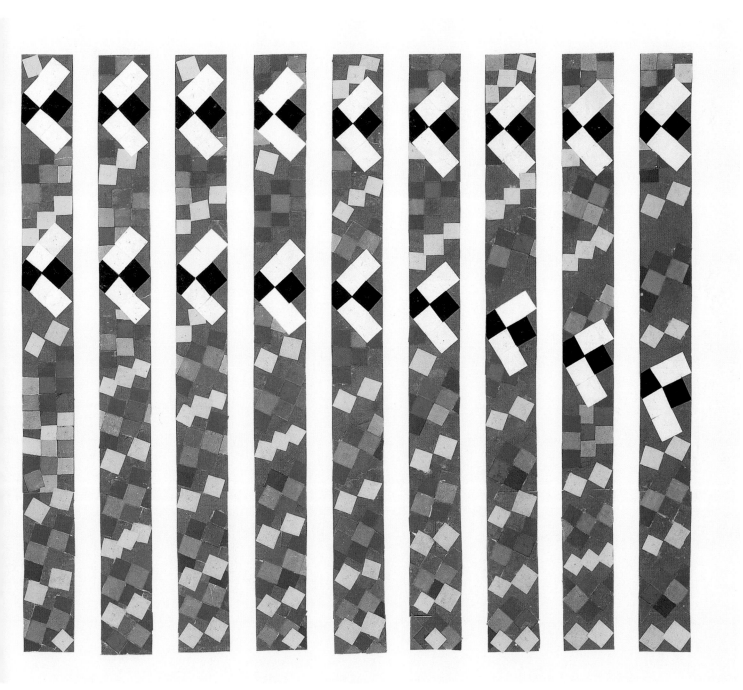

A tropical rainstorm!

Within a very short
time, three of the walls
are covered in water.

Matisse watches, delighted,
as several blue figures
dive into the water and
swim around like fish.
They float on their backs,
dive through the waves,
and leap like dolphins.

They remind Matisse of an exciting voyage he once made
twenty years ago to Tahiti and the island of Bora-Bora.

His scissors curve and circle through the paper,
flying like a bird in his hand.

The fine, white sand and a beautiful underwater paradise
—fish, starfish, whelks, little polyps and a whole world
of underwater plants—are all swimming on his walls.

The sea glitters in many colours. Green, red, orange and blue leaves and seaweed slowly sink towards the seabed. Between them, azure-blue fruit is floating around and, for a moment, a beautiful mermaid appears, dancing gracefully around the plants. A cheeky little parakeet flutters down from the wall and lands on the artist's shoulder, where it turns into a white dove.

Together, the artist and the bird gaze in admiration at the magnificent colours of the corals and the water— an ocean of brightly coloured seaweed as far as the eye can see. Matisse feels a thrill of pleasure, as though he had just seen something quite wonderful for the very first time in his life—curious, astonished, inspired and free of gloomy thoughts.

Now he knows what it is like to see the world through the eyes of a child!

"Scissors are a wonderful tool . . . ," whispers Matisse to the bird on his shoulder. "Working with paper and scissors is something I could really become interested in . . . I am growing to like making cut-outs more and more. Why didn't I think of this before?"

At last, night falls on Tahiti. The water of the sea turns a deep, dark blue. A black seaweed shape, strange and beautiful, appears for a moment, only to sink slowly down into the endless depths.

. . . snip-snip, snippety-snip . . .

Matisse then sets his scissors aside.

# About the artist

Henri Matisse was born in 1869 in Le Cateau-Cambrésis in the north-east of France. He decided to become an artist when he was twenty-one years old, and went to live in Paris. Travelling became more and more important to him, and he would sometimes go on journeys for several months, not just because he was fascinated by foreign countries and unfamiliar cultures, but also because he enjoyed meeting other artists, collectors and art lovers.

Paris   Switzerland   Morocco

Algeria   Tangiers   Antibes

Sweden   Italy   Tahiti

Moscow

Bora-Bora

London   Papeete

Issy   San Francisco

Spain   Florence

Venice   Bordeaux

Germany   Padua   Seville

Marseilles   New York

Berlin   Basle

Nice

Matisse's work was soon being shown in museums and galleries all over the world. By this time, he was travelling a lot between Paris, Issy-les-Moulineaux and the area around Nice, where he later lived at the Hotel Régina. His wife Amélie, their sons Jean and Pierre, and their daughter Marguerite, would often join him.

Matisse worked very hard. Even when he became old and frail and was too ill to leave his bed, he took every opportunity to turn his ideas into reality—when he was in bed, for example, he still managed to work on his cut-outs.

Matisse died in Nice in 1954. He was eighty-five years old.

"Basically, there is only Matisse," his friend Picasso once said. Perhaps Picasso meant that the perfection Matisse had reached in his art could hardly be topped. Some of Matisse's pictures are now so famous that they have simply become part of our lives. The wonderful lines and colours are familiar to many of us that we may somehow recognise them when we see them, even if we do not always remember the artist's name right away, or are not sure when or how they were made.

# What are cut-outs?

When the young Henri Matisse (who was working as a lawyer's assistant) had to spend almost a year in bed after a serious intestinal operation at the age of twenty-one, his mother Anna gave him a paintbox so that he would not get bored.

What a wonderful present!

That was how Matisse began a new life as an artist. Best of all, he liked to paint and draw landscapes, people and faces, but he also painted vases of flowers, bowls of fruit and even rooms.

Later, he liked trying to create pictures with as few lines and colours as possible. This was how he developed his special technique of cut-outs, which was a very important part of his work from the mid 1940s onwards. In fact, Matisse's famous cut-outs are often said to be his greatest works.

To make his cut-outs, Matisse would use scissors to cut shapes out of sheets of coloured paper. Then, he would arrange them very carefully to create a large picture and fix them to a surface—usually the walls of his room.

These works were the fulfilment of his life's dream: the perfect interaction of line and colour. Matisse no longer drew a person or object with a pencil and then coloured it in. Instead, he worked straight into the colour by cutting shapes out of sheets of coloured paper—just as a sculptor hews directly into stone in order to make a figure out of a formless block. In much the same way, Matisse uses only one colour, so that colour and form become one and the same.

Although we can always recognise the shapes Matisse makes, they are very simple compared to reality. For instance, when Matisse cuts out an apple, it does not look exactly like a real apple. It looks the way Matisse sees an apple. The cut-out figures and objects often form patterns which Matisse worked out very carefully and arranged to make a picture. Some of these works are huge—covering the wall of a room—while others are very small, as small as this page. All of them give us an idea of a beautiful paradise on earth, and show us how much Matisse loved life and enjoyed art.

# Make your own cut-outs

Do you want to have a go?
It really isn't difficult.
All you need is a pair of scissors and some coloured paper.

In order to get exactly the colour he wanted for his cut-outs,
Matisse mixed his own colours and used them to coat the paper.
This book contains a few sheets of paper in the same colours
that Matisse used.

What would you like to cut out?

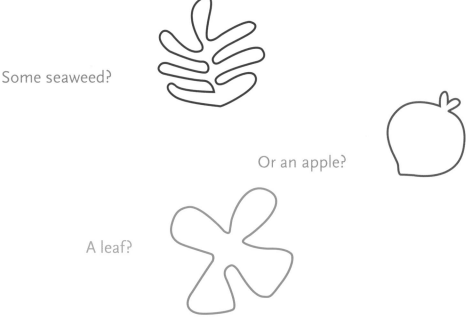

Some seaweed?

Or an apple?

A leaf?

Or something else?

Why not give it a try?

. . . snip-snip, snippety-snip . . .

snip-snip
snippety-snip

You can then stick the cut-outs onto a sheet of paper.
Or you might want to decorate the walls of your room with them.